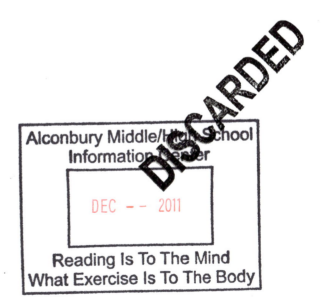

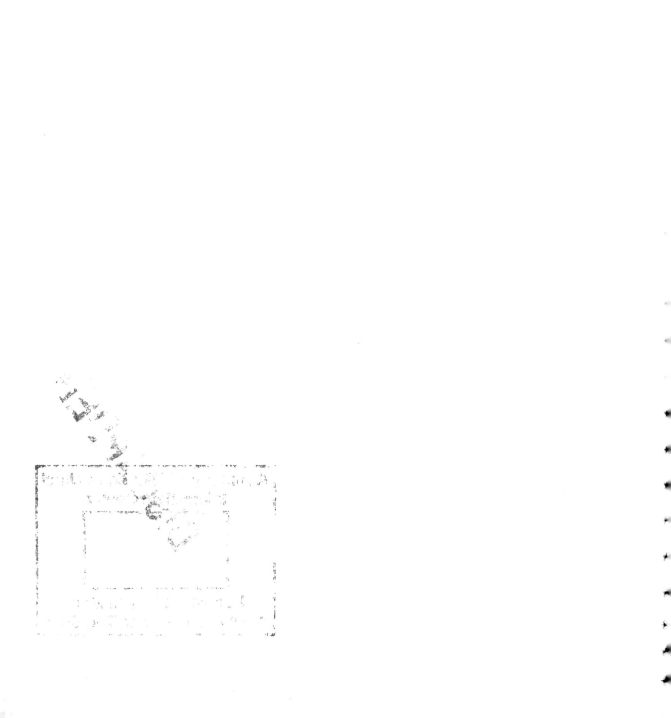

## DIGITAL AND INFORMATION LITERACY™

   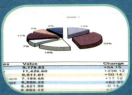

# CONSTRUCTING, USING, AND INTERPRETING SPREADSHEETS

PHILIP WOLNY

rosen publishing's
rosen central®

New York

Published in 2011 by The Rosen Publishing Group, Inc.
29 East 21st Street, New York, NY 10010

Copyright © 2011 by The Rosen Publishing Group, Inc.

First Edition

All rights reserved. No part of this book may be reproduced in any form without permission in writing from the publisher, except by a reviewer.

**Library of Congress Cataloging-in-Publication Data**

Wolny, Philip.
Constructing, using, and interpreting spreadsheets / Philip Wolny.—1st ed.
    p. cm.—(Digital and information literacy)
Includes bibliographical references and index.
ISBN 978-1-4358-9427-3 (library binding)
ISBN 978-1-4488-0595-2 (pbk)
ISBN 978-1-4488-0604-1 (6 pack)
1. Electronic spreadsheets—Juvenile literature. I. Title.
HF5548.2.W636 2011
005.54—dc22

2009050154

*Manufactured in the United States of America*

CPSIA Compliance Information: Batch #S10YA: For further information, contact Rosen Publishing, New York, New York, at 1-800-237-9932.

# CONTENTS

| | | |
|---|---|---|
| | Introduction | 4 |
| Chapter 1 | Spreadsheets: A Crash Course | 7 |
| Chapter 2 | Learning the Basics | 16 |
| Chapter 3 | The Mechanics: Setting Up Your Spreadsheet | 25 |
| Chapter 4 | Practical and Everyday Uses for Spreadsheets | 31 |
| | Glossary | 39 |
| | For More Information | 40 |
| | For Further Reading | 43 |
| | Bibliography | 44 |
| | Index | 46 |

# INTRODUCTION

Statistics, formulas, and data are all around us. If you stop and look closely, you'll realize just how important they are in everyday life. One of the most important parts of our lives in which we can examine the enormous usefulness of statistics, computation, record keeping, and planning is at school. Whether collecting and organizing names, phone numbers, and bus assignments for a school trip, or compiling and analyzing statistics from a winning basketball season, knowing how the numbers add up and what they mean is crucial. In the modern world, technology has given us an invaluable tool to calculate and manage numbers and other data: the electronic spreadsheet.

Let's imagine that a team or club at your school holds an annual fund-raising event to collect money for a local charity. Assume that last year, different groups of students raised money in different ways. While some students set up a car wash in the school parking lot, others managed a bake sale, while still others had a yard sale. Which groups raised the most money? Which fund-raising event was the most effective? How did the number of students working in each group affect the amount of money that was raised? What were each group's expenses versus its profits? Plugging such information into spreadsheets and analyzing the results could help next year's students decide on the most efficient ways to raise money.

Improving technology has made today's spreadsheets cheaper, easier to use, and more useful for multiple settings, including school, the office, and personal finances.

## CONSTRUCTING, USING, AND INTERPRETING SPREADSHEETS

From simple tasks, such as making a personal weekly budget, to more complicated projects and calculations, spreadsheets are not only useful, but sometimes impossible to live without in today's world. Using them in school activities now will prepare you for higher-level data projects in college. You'll also be prepared for a world in which almost every business uses spreadsheets in some way. And almost every employee must be familiar with the computer programs that create, operate, and maintain them. You are just as likely to encounter spreadsheets whether you work at a bank, run your own independent record label, or serve as a member of the U.S. military. Though some people may find spreadsheets intimidating, they are simpler than they look and are far more powerful and useful than they first appear.

In this book, we'll explore the ins and outs of electronic spreadsheets, dispel some myths about them, and see how they make our daily lives easier.

## Chapter 1

# Spreadsheets: A Crash Course

Long before computers revolutionized the way we live and work—in part, by making our planning, scheduling, record keeping, and mathematical computing far easier and more convenient—there was the paper worksheet. Paper worksheets were used by accountants and other financial professionals to track a company's or individual's income (money coming in) and expenses (money going out). But versions of the worksheet existed outside the office, too. A head of a household, for example, could track the living expenses for each member of the family on such a worksheet and compare it against the family income.

Generally, most calculations that people made were written out on hard copy. A business owner might use a book with lined sheets to do his or her bookkeeping. When it came to complicated calculations, a calculator was the best bet. The results of these calculations were written on oversized sheets of paper or in books called ledgers. They were often done across a two-page spread—that is, two pages facing each other—hence the term "spreadsheets."

# CONSTRUCTING, USING, AND INTERPRETING SPREADSHEETS

Before the personal computing revolution, business and personal finances were often done by hand. Here, a ruler and paper spreadsheet are used to check some calculations. Modern electronic spreadsheets have made such work much simpler and faster.

The first use of computerized spreadsheets for financial accounting dates back to 1961. That's when Professor Richard Mattessich wrote an academic paper that first described the basic principles behind digital spreadsheets. In 1969, Canadian computer programmers Rene Pardo and Remy Landau invented LANPAR (Language for Programming Arrays at Random), the first true spreadsheet program. It was mainly used for overseeing budgets by companies such as Bell Canada, AT&T, and General

SPREADSHEETS: A CRASH COURSE

Motors. But it would be another decade before spreadsheets would become available to small businesses and the general public.

## VisiCalc and the Personal Computing Revolution

Perhaps the first commercial spreadsheet for business and private consumers was VisiCalc, developed by Dan Bricklin and Bob Frankston. It was first released in 1979 for the Apple II computer. Its name is an abbreviation of "Visible Calculation" or "Visible Calculator." Computer experts and major corporations had used computer technology for many years to

VisiCalc's developers, Bob Frankston *(left)* and Dan Bricklin formed Software Arts Corporation in 1979 to further develop and sell their groundbreaking spreadsheet program.

## CONSTRUCTING, USING, AND INTERPRETING SPREADSHEETS

perform calculations and store data. Yet VisiCalc was revolutionary in two important ways.

In electronic form, the program created a digital worksheet that closely resembled a traditional paper-based worksheet. This made it visually familiar to those who had previously used traditional hard-copy spreadsheets and therefore was easier to use. The program was user friendly in another highly innovative way. Earlier spreadsheet programs and software had performed similar functions as VisiCalc, but they required the user to supply complex instructions written in code. One had to be familiar with programming languages in order to use them. VisiCalc was different. It was one of the earliest examples of the what you see is what you get (WYSIWYG) interface. With word-processing programs like Microsoft Word or WordPerfect, onscreen

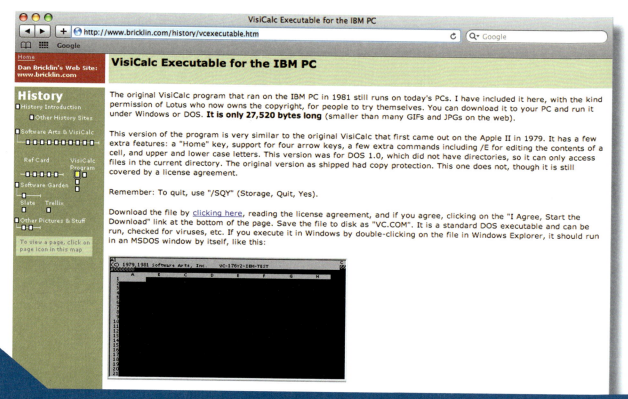

A page from Dan Bricklin's Web site (http://www.bricklin.com) provides a bit of history about VisiCalc and lets visitors sample the old software as it originally worked.

displays closely resembled the actual printed document that they were simulating. Similarly, with the new spreadsheet programs, you could enter numbers onscreen in the same way that you once penciled them in on paper.

Perhaps the most important new function that digital spreadsheets offered users was the ability to do calculations automatically. Instead of the user doing calculations mentally, on paper, or with the help of a calculator, and then entering the results, the program itself did automatic calculations. Initially, functions were simple ones, such as addition, subtraction, multiplication, and division. Another useful function was determining the average of a series, or group, of numbers. This allowed accountants to determine a company's average annual expenditures or the average salary of its managers. It could help them calculate average company earnings over the past decade and chart any upward or downward trends.

Spreadsheets could help track the average earnings of each of the company's divisions, so it could determine which divisions were performing well and which were struggling. They could even calculate the average length of employment of each division's employees, alerting executives to any division that seemed to lose employees quickly and might therefore need a change in management.

## Spreadsheets Enter the Home

In January 1983, Lotus 1-2-3 was launched as the newest spreadsheet offering. It ran on IBM PCs (personal computers), which were a new phenomenon at the time. The popularity of Lotus 1-2-3 actually helped drive an explosion in sales for IBM's computers. Very quickly, Lotus 1-2-3 became the industry standard. Its name came from the three main utilities it offered: spreadsheets, the ability to make charts and graphs, and some database capabilities.

When Microsoft introduced its hugely influential and popular Windows operating system a few years later, it also created software for that operating system. While Microsoft first developed the spreadsheet program Excel for Macintosh computers in 1985, it also released a version for Windows in 1987. Excel became the most widely used spreadsheet in

# CONSTRUCTING, USING, AND INTERPRETING SPREADSHEETS

Spreadsheet programs are so popular that there is a brisk trade in pirated software. Thomas Lemberg, a software lawyer, is seen here with computers displaying real and pirated copies of Lotus 1-2-3 software.

the world, with versions available for almost every brand of computer made. Nowadays, Excel is part of the Microsoft Office software package, which includes programs for word processing and graphics presentations, among other tools.

By the 1990s, computers had begun to enter almost all areas of American life—the office, the home, personal communication, entertainment, shopping, research, and reference. As they became more widespread, computers and software became cheaper. They were now affordable for

## Spreadsheets, Suites, and Compatibility

While there are spreadsheet programs that are sold and used as individual programs, many popular spreadsheets in use are included, or "bundled," with other computer software. A product line or family that allows you to perform a variety of tasks with your computer is sometimes referred to as a "suite." Microsoft Office, for example, is a suite of products that works with the Windows operating system, though it's also produced for other systems. Office includes not just Excel, but also Microsoft Word for word processing and PowerPoint for presentations. Lotus 1-2-3 works especially well with other Lotus software products, while Quattro Pro is part of the WordPerfect suite.

For a long time, it was industry practice that software companies designed software to work on specific operating systems on particular computers. In recent years, there have been many improvements in making different programs from various companies work well together. Some free software (such as OpenOffice, with its Calc spreadsheet) is intentionally designed to work with other computer programs written by different companies.

small businesses and ordinary households. Spreadsheets quickly became one of the most widely used tools in American business. Knowing how to use them was now an important skill for almost anyone entering the workforce. Today, students can begin learning how to use spreadsheets starting in grade school. They can refine their skills and master more complex utilities in high school, technical school, and college. Knowing how to create, maintain, and interpret spreadsheets is a valuable set of skills to learn and have on one's résumé.

# CONSTRUCTING, USING, AND INTERPRETING SPREADSHEETS

Some spreadsheet programs work best with compatible computer operating systems. Yet these systems often do not come bundled with software, which must be purchased separately. For those who can't afford top-of-the-line spreadsheet programs, freeware is a legitimate option.

# Freeware: The Right Price

Today, there are many options available for those who want to use spreadsheets. There are the most popular and well-known spreadsheet programs—namely Microsoft Excel, Lotus 1-2-3, and WordPerfect Office's Quattro Pro. For businesses, educators, and other professionals, a well-established spreadsheet program, whether or not it is part of a larger suite or set of software, might be the best bet. These programs can be pricey, however, especially for students.

If someone is on a budget, or simply wants to learn the basics before committing to a spreadsheet program, there are various free spreadsheets, or freeware (free software), available for download online. A quick Internet search for free downloadable spreadsheet programs yields many possibilities.

Finally, you don't even need to download a program to your computer to enjoy the benefits of spreadsheets. Increasingly, there are Web-based spreadsheet programs available. All you need is an Internet connection and a browser. The user simply goes to the provider's Web site and works on a spreadsheet online. The user can then save his or her work onto the computer's hard drive or onto the provider's server. Google, Inc.'s Google Docs spreadsheets program is one example, but there are more in development every day.

Remember, however, that you must use extreme caution when downloading programs, files, and other materials from the Internet. To protect your computer from viruses, spyware, and other intrusions, do some research before downloading any programs, especially free ones. See if users have complained about any spyware or malware that was attached to the programs. Also, make sure what you are pulling off the Internet is a full-fledged spreadsheet program and not a "Trojan horse" that will sneak in through a virus or other spyware and malware. Knowledgeable adults, like teachers and consumer product reviewers, should offer valuable, reliable, and insightful opinions on the best spreadsheet options available to you.

## Chapter 2

# Learning the Basics

So you've just opened a new spreadsheet document, blank, untouched, and ready to be filled with data. The first thing you will probably notice is the layout. Spreadsheets typically have several parts to them. At the top, you usually have the title of your document.

## Menu and Toolbars

Typically, the menu bar sits just beneath the spreadsheet's title. This is usually a drop-down menu. That is, each menu item expands, dropping down into a longer list of more specific options when you click on it.

Just below the menu bar, a series of buttons or icons make up the toolbar. Many of these perform specific actions, which the user can perform by single-clicking on them. Examples include opening a new document or folder, saving a document, inserting or deleting elements like text or graphics, and so forth. Many spreadsheet toolbars also include formatting buttons, with which you can change fonts by style or size.

LEARNING THE BASICS

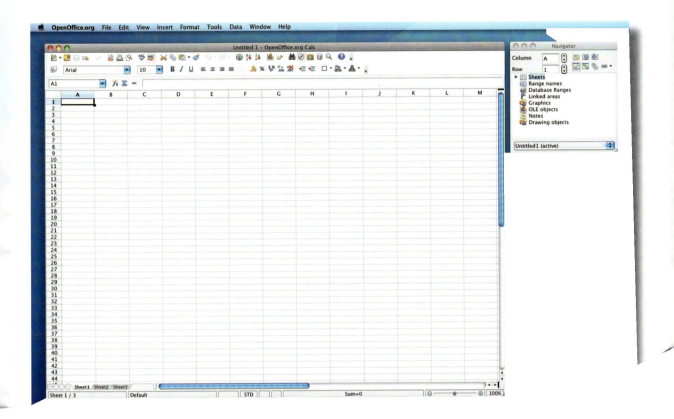

# On the Grid: Columns and Rows

Below the menu and toolbars are the nuts and bolts of the spreadsheet. This is the numerical grid where numbers and other elements are displayed and calculations are performed. The elements listed in the grid going from left to right at the top of a spreadsheet are known as columns. The elements going top to bottom along the side of a spreadsheet are known as rows.

## CONSTRUCTING, USING, AND INTERPRETING SPREADSHEETS

Generally, a new or blank spreadsheet will have columns represented sequentially (that is, in order) by letters. Thus, the first column will be A, the second one B, the third C, and so forth. Similarly, rows are listed numerically, starting at 1 and continuing to 2, 3, 4, and so on. When you start doing more complex work with spreadsheets, you can rename these elements. For example, if you were tracking the school baseball team's stats, each row could be a player's name. And column A could be at-bats, column B hits, column C batting average, etc.

The columns and rows produce the grid into which you plug your information. If you run your mouse down column A to where it hits the second row, you will be at the intersection of A and 2. This intersection, represented as a box, is known as a cell. Its cell reference, or name, is A2. A spreadsheet with ten columns and ten rows will have one hundred cells in it.

When you open a spreadsheet, the highlighted cell will always be A1, the cell highest up and farthest to the left on the grid. A dark border tells you that this is the selected, highlighted, or active cell. To move to another cell, you can use your mouse to click anywhere on the grid. You can also use the arrow keys toward the bottom-right area of your keyboard to go up, down, left, or right.

## Using Formulas

Take a look above the spreadsheet's grid at the section just below the toolbar. This is the formula bar. The formula bar sometimes has an adjacent one-click icon next to it that drops down into a list of standard formulas.

The formula bar is one of the most powerful spreadsheet tools because it gives you the ability to do calculations quickly and automatically. It is one of several things that you, the user, add to the spreadsheet to make it useful. To get some practice with these formulas, we will set up a very basic, introductory spreadsheet and use it to perform some simple tasks.

Pretend that you and three other friends (Don, Mike, and Sarah) are tracking your grades in six different subjects (math, English, science, social

LEARNING THE BASICS

studies, health, and art) throughout the school year. You would like to find out the average grade for each subject among the four students, as well as each student's overall grade average for the six classes.

Your first step is to name the rows 1 to 6 after your six subjects, and then name the columns (A, B, C, and D) after yourself and your three friends. Next, input each student's grades in each subject in the appropriate cells. These grades are called values. Values in spreadsheets are any numbers,

# CONSTRUCTING, USING, AND INTERPRETING SPREADSHEETS

dates, amounts, or other data that you input into cells. Plug the grades into the cells from A1 to D6.

The next steps are to calculate and show the results on the spreadsheet. To figure out an overall grade average for one of the four students, for instance, the most logical way would be to create a row at the bottom. Skip down a couple of cells below your last subject and label that row "Overall Average." In that row, move to the cell in the column of your first friend. Here's where you will insert your first formula—an average of his or her grades in the six courses.

## Calculating an Average

The value you want for this selected cell will be the average of all of Friend #1's subject grades, listed in cells A1, A2, A3, and so forth. You can calculate the average in two different ways.

First, you can go to the toolbar and select Insert. Then scroll down to Function and pick Average out of that drop-down menu. The characters AVERAGE (number 1, number 2 . . .) will appear in the box. In the parenthesis, you select which series of cells you want to figure out the average for. In this case, it will be cells A1 through A6, so you type "A1:A6" in the parenthesis. The colon is another way of expressing the words "from/to" (i.e. "From A1 to A6"). Any group of cells, whether merely two in a row or several hundred, is known as a range. In this case, the range we wish to average is A1–A6 (Friend #1's grades). Adding a closing parenthesis finishes the formula, and hitting enter or return activates it. Note that the average of Friend #1's subject grades has been automatically computed and placed in the appropriate cell. Then move on to Friend #2's grades (cells B1–B6) and so on.

Another way to find an average of selected values is to click on the first cell. Then hold down the Shift key and scroll down with the arrow key or with your mouse. This allows you to highlight and select a range of cells. With these cells selected, you can use the menu bar to insert an "Average"

LEARNING THE BASICS

If you are trying to figure out grade averages for your classes, it might help to input them into a spreadsheet every time you receive the results of a test or assignment. Later, you can easily calculate this information using the spreadsheet's Average formula.

formula, as described above. The formula is then inserted in the empty cell beneath the range of cells you are calculating. The result of the computation—the average of those highlighted and selected values—will appear in that cell.

Having computed each student's average grade among the six courses, you can now try to figure out the average grade among the four students for each course (science, math, etc.). In this case, you will be averaging the range of values in the cells A1–D1 (science grades for each of the four students), then A2–D2 (math grades for each of the four students), and so on. Use the fifth column (E1–E6) to show your results—the average grade for each subject.

## Additional Functions and Formulas

In addition to figuring out averages, there are several other simple functions and formulas that you can use in spreadsheets. As you become more experienced and comfortable with spreadsheets, you can create and use ever more complex ones.

Many of the most popular and useful spreadsheet functions and formulas are also the simplest. For example, you can add the values of a range of cells using the SUM function. This would be useful in a spreadsheet devoted to tracking the amount of money you make each week from your after-school job. If you're saving up for a new video game and are unsure if you have enough money yet, all you have to do is highlight the cells indicating your past month's paper route income and hit SUM.

There are also functions for the subtracting, multiplying, and dividing of values in your spreadsheet. If you have a bigger range of values and you want to quickly show the maximum or minimum values in that range, you can use the MAX or MIN functions. In a spreadsheet listing the grade point averages (GPAs) of every student in your grade, you can easily isolate the highest GPA using the MAX function. Similarly, you can quickly locate the lowest GPA with the MIN function. Someone may want to do this to determine which student has the highest GPA and deserves an academic award, or which student has the lowest GPA and needs some extra help or tutoring.

## The Sky's the Limit, Almost

In the end, the calculations your spreadsheet can do are limited only by your imagination. There are limits, however, to the amount of information that you can plug into a single spreadsheet. Excel, for example, has a maximum number of rows (65,536) and columns (256). While rows are in numerical order, columns go from A to Z, and then continue as Aa, Ab, Ac, and so on. The chances are slim, however, that students will need anywhere near that number of cells for most projects or tasks. But professionals in many careers often manage enormous amounts of data that make it necessary to completely fill up such spreadsheets.

**CONSTRUCTING, USING, AND INTERPRETING SPREADSHEETS**

# MYTHS & FACTS

**MYTH** Spreadsheets are difficult to use. Only people with technical skills are able to use them well.

**FACT** Spreadsheets are very straightforward, and you can do a lot with them as a beginner. You don't need to be a mathematical whiz to become comfortable with spreadsheets. Many people who use them are not particularly good at math. The spreadsheet programs do the math for you. That is why they are so convenient and valuable.

**MYTH** You need to learn spreadsheets only if you are choosing a career like accounting or banking.

**FACT** Spreadsheets are useful—and used—in nearly any job or profession and in many aspects of our daily lives. It is now generally assumed among college educators and employers that you will know how to create, use, and analyze spreadsheets.

**MYTH** You can only purchase a good spreadsheet program bundled with other programs that you may not need or be able to afford in an "office suite" or package.

**FACT** While the better-known spreadsheets are available for purchase as part of larger office program packages, there is a huge variety of spreadsheet programs available for download or online use. By shopping around, you can find one that is right for you.

# Chapter 3

# The Mechanics: Setting Up Your Spreadsheet

Spreadsheets offer a great deal of power when it comes to calculating numbers and analyzing the results of these calculations. In this chapter, we will look at some of the ways we can use that power effectively. We will also explore how we can format our spreadsheets to our liking.

## Constants and Formulas

When entering information into the cells of a spreadsheet, there are two types that are input: constants and formulas. A "constant" refers to an entry that does not change. It could be a number, such as the value of a student's exam score or a date. It can be descriptive text, such as a student's name or the name of a month (in the case of an annual budget).

A formula often combines arithmetic operators (like +, -, *, /) and numeric constants. The formula you choose tells the spreadsheet program what to do with the values you place in the cells (average them out, for example, or simply add or subtract them).

CONSTRUCTING, USING, AND INTERPRETING SPREADSHEETS

# Inserting and Deleting Rows and Columns

Sometimes the project you are working on requires you to make changes to the spreadsheet. The elements you are measuring or displaying may vary over time. In the student grade spreadsheet example from the previous chapter, you may want to add a column for the results of a recent test. Or perhaps a new student has joined the study group, or one of the original four students has left. What do you do if, say, two people join the group and one person leaves? These simple spreadsheet revisions can be performed in just a few steps.

First, go to the students' names. Scroll over to the name of the person leaving the group and click above it on the lettered column. This selects the entire column, which you can then delete, often by right-clicking and then selecting Delete, or by performing the same action using the toolbar.

When designing a spreadsheet, remember how important legibility is. A spreadsheet that is difficult to use and read may lead to misinterpreted information and poorly understood results.

Next, select a column next to which you would like to insert new columns (for the two new students). You can either use the toolbar or right-click on a cell. In some drop-down menus, you will have the option of inserting columns to the right or left of the selected one. Insert two columns where you prefer. Then you can add the relevant grades for each of the new students in each course.

## Inserting or Deleting Individual Cells

Sometimes you will only want to add or delete an individual cell, not an entire row or column. To do this, you need to select a cell above or next to where you want the new cell to be inserted. After pulling down the Insert menu, select Cells, which opens a dialog box. Here you have the option

of shifting cells right or down. To delete a cell, you have to select the Edit menu, and pick Delete. To shift cells left or up, you need to click the option button.

What is the best way to learn your way around spreadsheets? Just try doing different things, plugging in new values, or tinkering with different formulas and functions, and you will start to get the hang of it quicker than you think. Have fun experimenting with the program. Be creative in trying to devise new spreadsheets that track various kinds of data: upcoming album releases and concerts by your favorite bands; your monthly income (earnings) and expenses (costs); your Girl Scout cookie sales, broken down by day of the week and type of cookie; an exercise schedule broken down by day and activity, perhaps with columns for Calories Burned and Duration (time); etc.

# Formatting and Layout: Changing the Spreadsheet's Look and Feel

Making a spreadsheet easy to read and interpret is an important goal and crucial skill to develop. If someone can't make sense of your spreadsheet's organization or use of information, your data will be meaningless to him or her. There are many ways to format and lay out your information so that it is clear and comprehensible.

## Changing Width and Height

Sometimes you will have enough room in your spreadsheet's cells for all the information you wish to insert within them. Other times, you will not. If the names for your column headers are very long, for example, or the data you wish to enter in cells under that column is lengthy, only a portion of the information will appear in the standard-size column cells. To expand the width of a column and its cells, you can select a column, click on the Format menu, and select Column and then Width.

A default width in Excel is 10, meaning that you can fit ten characters in ten-point Helvetica font in a cell of standard width. You can also use the Best Fit function here to have each column automatically adjust to your data, regardless of width.

## Fonts: Styles, Size, and Alignment

Ideally, spreadsheets present information in as straightforward a manner as possible. That is why it is vital to pick appropriate fonts, font styles, and font sizes, and to choose logically how to align your columns and rows. The choices you make can help someone who is viewing your spreadsheet. The easier someone can read, understand, and interpret your data and what you are trying to do with that data, the more successful your spreadsheet will be.

The formatting toolbar in spreadsheet programs is often similar—sometimes nearly identical, actually—to toolbars in word processing or other programs. Most spreadsheets have a default font and font size that you start with when working in each newly opened document. Naturally, you can change this default setting if it is not to your liking or doesn't suit your data and purposes. To change the program's default formatting, the formatting toolbar generally offers a choice of fonts, font sizes, and several other buttons that automatically change the style of the text. Default text is plain, but you can change the setting to make it bold, italicized, or underlined.

Picking an appropriate font size and proper alignment is important because it can make the spreadsheet easier to read and decipher. You will find that if you are dealing with very large numbers, it might be easier to space them out across the page or screen. On the other hand, you may need to fit a great deal of data on a single sheet, and things could get cramped. Presenting your data so that it is highly readable, fits comfortably within the cells, and does not looked crammed on the page is crucial to your spreadsheet's success. This is why plain type, which is not bold, and a smaller font size is usually preferable, and the program's default settings are often the best in most ordinary circumstances.

**CONSTRUCTING, USING, AND INTERPRETING SPREADSHEETS**

# TEN GREAT QUESTIONS
## TO ASK A DIGITAL LIBRARIAN

1. What are some good information sources and online tutorials that I can use to learn more about spreadsheets?

2. How do spreadsheets help save time?

3. What are the differences, if any, between spreadsheet freeware and spreadsheet programs that one needs to purchase?

4. If I don't have access to spreadsheets at home, where in my community can I access, learn how to use, and create spreadsheets?

5. Where can I take classes on designing and using spreadsheets, whether at my school, a community organization, or a local community or technical college?

6. What are some of the ways that I can present the raw data in my spreadsheet in another, more visual format, such as a chart or other graphic organizer?

7. What are a few of the more obvious advantages of using spreadsheets to perform calculations instead of doing them by hand or with a calculator?

8. What are some of the criteria that you use to decide what kinds of information to include in a spreadsheet and whether these elements should be represented in columns or in rows?

9. What are some useful and current reference books and higher-level online tutorials that help the user improve his or her working knowledge of spreadsheets, using challenging practice exercises?

10. What is the difference between spreadsheet programs and accounting software?

## Chapter 4

# Practical and Everyday Uses for Spreadsheets

Spreadsheets can be used for very specific purposes. We can be creative in how we use spreadsheets by adding meaningful elements to them. By doing so, we can connect different facts gathered from research and observation, analyze them, and use them to make real-world decisions.

For example, one can design a spreadsheet to show how a group of students performs on several quizzes and tests during a semester of math class. The results of this grade tracking can help instructors determine if their teaching methods are working, if the tests are too difficult or too easy, which students need extra help, and which sections of the math curriculum are giving students the most trouble.

## Spreadsheet Science

Since it is underpinned by numbers, measurements, quantitative observation, and other kinds of "hard" data, one of the more obvious spreadsheet-friendly

# CONSTRUCTING, USING, AND INTERPRETING SPREADSHEETS

Spreadsheets are especially useful in precise numbers-oriented subject areas such as math and science. Here, some students in a science class take notes on an experiment. Their data can be put into a spreadsheet to record and analyze the details of the experiment and its outcome.

subjects is science. Imagine that your biology class has begun a section on botany, the study of plant life.

The class is divided into several groups of students. Each group must grow a plant over a few months' time. Each group is assigned different amounts of soil, water, and other supplies. Because each group is using different quantities and ratios of these materials, the various plants could be expected to grow at different rates. Every group creates and maintains a spreadsheet to chart the quantities of water, soil, light, and other nutrients used and how often they are used or applied over a thirty-day period. The spreadsheet also charts the plant's rate of growth day to day.

At the end of the thirty days, the group whose plant shows the greatest rate of growth could be considered the one who had used the optimum amounts and ratios of soil, water, light, etc. That group's spreadsheet would provide a record of how and when the care and feeding were provided, what the optimum ratios were, and how much the plant grew as a result. The other groups' spreadsheets would also help clarify which growing techniques and nutrient ratios worked fairly well and which didn't encourage the plants' growth and health.

## Spreadsheet Geography

Other subject areas where you might use spreadsheets are social studies or geography. Your teacher may ask you to design a spreadsheet comparing different nations around the world. Imagine that you have to compare the populations and population density between dry, desert countries and wet, tropical ones.

Using trusted sources on the Internet or reference books from a library, your spreadsheet might include the average rainfall, population, population density, urban vs. rural populations, and country area, or size, for each nation included in the study. Your teacher might assign you the task of figuring out how to calculate population density in your spreadsheet—that is, how many people per square mile (or square kilometer) live in a place.

## CONSTRUCTING, USING, AND INTERPRETING SPREADSHEETS

You would be devising a formula that divides the number of people in the nation by the nation's area (measured in square miles or kilometers).

Your teacher could grade your spreadsheet on several criteria: whether the formula you employed for population density was correct, how clearly you organized the information on your spreadsheet, if all pertinent data relating to population and climate were included, and how easy it is to

SPREADSHEETS TO THE RESCUE!

## Spreadsheets to the Rescue!

To illustrate the real-world utility of spreadsheets, let's take a look at all the members of your school's marching band. Let's assume we make a spreadsheet that tracks all the results of their quizzes and tests in all classes throughout the semester. We notice that both excellent and average students do worse on certain tests given at certain times. If we follow up and determine what was happening in or out of school on those "bad" test days, we may discover that those tests fell on the day of or the day before a big football game for which the band was preparing its performance.

    Discovering this connection between raw test data and outside events may influence teachers' decisions about what days to give tests or may influence band members to form study groups—or at least set aside extra study time before big games. Spreadsheets help us make these kinds of cause-and-effect connections that might remain invisible otherwise. And they help us make the wisest decisions about how to use the data recorded in them to achieve the best results in the real world.

draw a conclusion based on your spreadsheet results. By quickly scanning your spreadsheet, can someone draw an accurate conclusion about how climate affects population (i.e. arid countries tend to be less populous, and the population is more clustered in urban areas)? What could you have done differently? Did you include or exclude things your classmates left in or took out?

## CONSTRUCTING, USING, AND INTERPRETING SPREADSHEETS

No longer confined just to desktops or laptops, spreadsheet applications, or apps, are also coming out for smartphones and other portable devices, like this Apple iPad.

## Beyond Calculation

Because spreadsheets are relatively easy to use and are flexible, you can design them for a variety of uses, many of them not involving calculations. Often, they can be used as databases or lists. If you are going on a class trip, for example, your teacher may collect the cell phone numbers of all students, chaperones, and students' emergency contacts, and have them ready on a spreadsheet printout. Spreadsheets could also be used to present a visual timetable for such a trip or create a lesson plan or schedule for the day's activities. They can also be a convenient tool to create calendars, or weekly planners, for both students and educators.

A teacher might also have a spreadsheet listing contact information for all his or her students' parents. A spreadsheet record of grades for a semester's worth of classwork might simply list grades or other information, rather than actually be used to calculate anything specific, such as averages or highest and lowest scores.

## Charts and Graphs

While a spreadsheet can tell you a great deal, you can increase its impact by translating its raw listing of data into a more visual, reader-friendly, and quickly comprehensible format. A pie chart that divides world population among the continents, for example, might give you a better and more immediate understanding of the world's population distribution than columns of percentages in a spreadsheet would.

Many spreadsheets have toolbar menu options and other features that allow you to express your spreadsheet data visually. In Excel, for instance, you can select a group of values, or a whole spreadsheet, and click the icon for the Chart Wizard. This opens a dialog box that allows you to pick from among different types of charts and graphs into which you can translate your spreadsheet data.

If you have room in your document, you can even select the "As Object In" option for your chart or graph. This allows you to have your spreadsheet and its corresponding chart or graph appear side by side. In Quattro Pro, you can pick a similar option by using the Graph drop-down menu.

## The Spreadsheet: A Powerful Tool

You have seen how spreadsheets can be an effective tool in classrooms, for school assignments, and even at home. Depending on what kind of career you choose, you may encounter their use quite often in everyday life.

## CONSTRUCTING, USING, AND INTERPRETING SPREADSHEETS

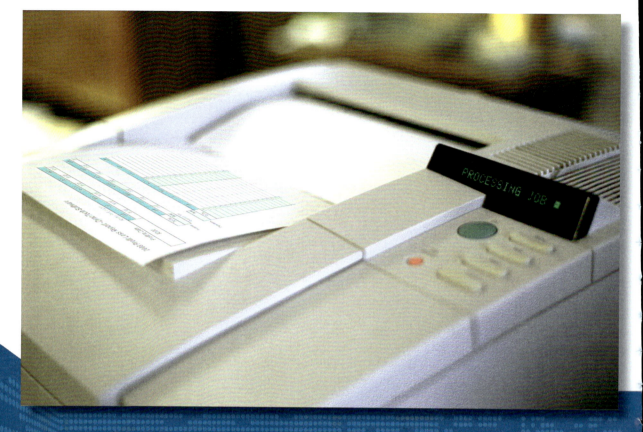

Electronic spreadsheets do not exist only on screen. They can be printed out and read, interpreted, shared, and presented as hard copies for use in meetings, presentations, or written reports.

Spreadsheets are used in marketing, accounting, banking, military and law enforcement, health care, government, education, and countless other jobs and professions. If you get a head start on their use, you will become comfortable and skilled with an invaluable tool that simplifies so many types of work and projects. This knowledge will make you very attractive to a prospective employer. Whatever direction your career and education take, it is a good bet that spreadsheets will figure in somehow. So get started working—and having fun—with them today!

# GLOSSARY

**active cell**  The cell in a spreadsheet document that is currently selected and into which information is being entered.

**cell**  The intersection of a column and a row in a spreadsheet document.

**cell reference**  The use of another cell's address in a formula.

**column**  The vertical dimension or reference of a spreadsheet.

**fill handle**  In an active cell, the square at the lower right-hand corner that can be used to copy or expand formulas or numeric progressions into neighboring cells.

**formula**  A mathematical equation that uses spreadsheet data to yield certain results.

**formula bar**  An area of the spreadsheet application's window that displays the contents of the active cell, including formulas.

**function**  A pre-established formula that you can use to perform calculations. Some spreadsheets have dozens of standard formulas that are ready for use at the click of a mouse.

**range**  A selection of cells.

**row**  The horizontal dimension or reference of a spreadsheet.

**selecting**  Choosing and highlighting a group of cells.

**toolbar**  The series of buttons and icons at the top of a spreadsheet document used to perform a variety of actions.

**workbook**  In Excel, the name of a spreadsheet document.

**worksheet**  In Excel, the different pages, or sheets, that can make up a workbook.

**WYSIWYG**  An acronym standing for "What you see is what you get," referring to visual content displayed in computer applications that looks more or less identical to its finished product; for example, a printed word-processing document closely resembles the "virtual" document that you see on-screen.

# FOR MORE INFORMATION

American Accounting Association
5717 Bessie Drive
Sarasota, FL 34233-2399
(941) 921-7747
Web site: http://aaahq.org
The American Accounting Association promotes worldwide excellence in accounting education, research, and practice.

Computers for Youth
322 Eighth Avenue, Floor 12A
New York, NY 10001
(212) 563-7300
Web site: http://www.cfy.org
Computers for Youth provides inner-city students with home computers and training, technical support, and online training so that they can do better in school.

Educational Computing Organization of Ontario
10 Morrow Avenue, Suite 202
Toronto, ON M6R 2J1
Canada
(416) 489-1713
Web site: http://www.ecoo.org
The Educational Computing Organization of Ontario helps teachers and students incorporate computer learning into the educational process.

Get Net Wise
Internet Education Foundation
1634 I Street NW

FOR MORE INFORMATION

Washington, DC 20009
Web site: http://www.getnetwise.org
Get Net Wise is part of the Internet Education Foundation, which works to provide a safe online environment for children and families.

International Society for Technology in Education (ISTE)
1710 Rhode Island Avenue NW, Suite 900
Washington, DC 20036
(866) 654-4777
Web site: http://www.iste.org
ISTE works to improve teaching, learning, and school leadership by advancing the effective use of technology in pre-kindergarten to twelfth grade and teacher education.

Internet Education Foundation
1634 I Street NW, Suite 1100
Washington, DC 20006
(202) 637-0968
Web site: http://neted.org
The Internet Education Foundation is a nonprofit organization dedicated to informing the public about Internet education.

Just Think
39 Mesa Street, Suite 106
San Francisco, CA 94129
(415) 561-2900
Web site: http://justthink.org
Just Think is a nonprofit foundation that promotes media literacy for young people.

Media Awareness Network
1500 Merivale Road, 3rd Floor
Ottawa, ON K2E 6Z5
Canada
(613) 224-7721
Web site: http://www.media-awareness.ca
The Media Awareness Network creates media literacy programs for young Canadians. The site contains educational games about the Internet and media.

Microsoft Corporation
One Microsoft Way
Redmond, WA 98052
(425) 882-8080
Web site: http://www.microsoft.com
Microsoft developed and manufactures the Excel spreadsheet program as part of its Office applications suite. It is the leading spreadsheet on the world market.

## Web Sites

Due to the changing nature of Internet links, Rosen Publishing has developed an online list of Web sites related to the subject of this book. This site is updated regularly. Please use this link to access the list:

http://www.rosenlinks.com/dil/spre

# FOR FURTHER READING

Harvey, Greg. *Excel 2007 All-in-One Desk Reference for Dummies.* Hoboken, NJ: Wiley Publishing, Inc., 2007.

Harvey, Greg. *Excel 2007 for Dummies.* Hoboken, NJ: Wiley Publishing, Inc., 2006.

Hawthorn, Kate. *A Young Person's Guide to the Internet.* New York, NY: Routledge, 2005.

Hayde, Yvonne. *Easy Everyday Excel 2007.* Chandler, AZ: Copadego Publishing, 2008.

Hayden, Yvonne. *So You Need to Make a Spreadsheet.* Chandler, AZ: Copadego Publishing, 2006.

Hock, Randolph. *The Extreme Searcher's Internet Handbook.* 2nd ed. Medford, NJ: CyberAge Books, 2007.

Jacoby, Carol. *Simple Spreadsheets for Hard Decisions.* Long Beach, CA: City Shore Press, 2008.

Lewis, Pamela. *Spreadsheet Magic.* 2nd ed. Washington, DC: International Society for Technology in Education, 2006.

Marmel, Elaine. *Absolute Beginner's Guide to Quattro Pro X3.* Don Mills, ON, Canada: Que Publishing/Pearson Technology Publishing Group, 2006.

Milton, Michael. *Head First Excel: A Learner's Guide to Spreadsheets.* Sebastopol, CA: O'Reilly Media, 2010.

Shaw, Maura D. *Mastering Online Research.* Cincinnati, OH: Writer's Digest Books, 2007.

Tidrow, Rob, and Eric Otchet. *IBM Lotus Symphony for Dummies.* Hoboken, NJ: Wiley Publishing, Inc., 2008.

# BIBLIOGRAPHY

Bender, Eric. "Three Minutes: Godfathers of the Spreadsheet." *PC World*, June 3, 2004. Retrieved August 2009 (http://www.pcworld.com/article/116166/three_minutes_godfathers_of_the_spreadsheet.html).

Biersdorfer, J. D. "Cracking Open a Spreadsheet." *New York Times*, August 16, 2007. Retrieved August 2009 (http://www.nytimes.com/2007/08/16/technology/circuits/16askk-001.html).

Ericson, Richard. "Hands On: Google Spreadsheets Is More Powerful Than You Think." *Computerworld*, June 9, 2006. Retrieved September 2009 (http://www.computerworld.com/s/article/print/9001087/Hands_on_Google_Spreadsheets_is_more_powerful_than_you_think).

Fitzsimmons, Caitlin. "Why on Earth Would I Want an Online Spreadsheet?" *Guardian UK*, June 8, 2006. Retrieved July 2009 (http://www.guardian.co.uk/technology/2006/jun/08/guardianweeklytechnologysection).

Gottesman, Ben Z. "Beyond Numbers: Manipulating Text in Excel." *PC Mag*, May 21, 2009. Retrieved July 2009 (http://www.pcmag.com/article2/0,2817,2347461,00.asp).

Grauer, Robert T., Michelle Hulett, Cynthia Krebs, Maurie Lockley, and Judy Scheeren. *Exploring Microsoft Office 2007 Plus Edition*. Upper Saddle River, NJ: Prentice Hall, 2007.

Har-Even, Benny. "30 Years of the Spreadsheet." *IT Pro*, June 12, 2009. Retrieved September 2009 (http://www.itpro.co.uk/611644/30-years-of-the-spreadsheet).

Harvey, Greg. *Excel 2007 All-in-One Desk Reference for Dummies*. Hoboken, NJ: Wiley Publishing, Inc., 2007.

Harvey, Greg. *Excel 2007 for Dummies*. Hoboken, NJ: Wiley Publishing, Inc., 2006.

Lewis, Peter H. "The Executive Computer; Lotus 1-2-3 Faces Up to the Upstarts." *New York Times*, March 13, 1988. Retrieved September

2009 (http://www.nytimes.com/1988/03/13/business/the-executive-computer-lotus-1-2-3-faces-up-to-the-upstarts.html).

Marmel, Elaine. *Absolute Beginner's Guide to Quattro Pro X3*. Don Mills, ON, Canada: Que Publishing/Pearson Technology Publishing Group, 2006.

Microsoft.com. "Help for Excel 2007." Retrieved September 2009 (http://office.microsoft.com/en-us/excel/FX100646951033.aspx).

Milton, Michael. *Head First Excel: A Learner's Guide to Spreadsheets*. Sebastopol, CA: O'Reilly Media, 2010.

North Carolina Public Schools. "Almost Everything You Need for Using Spreadsheets in the Classroom." NCWiseOwl.org. Retrieved September 2009 (http://www.ncwiseowl.org/kscope/techknowpark/freefall/resources.html).

Tidrow, Rob, and Eric Otchet. *IBM Lotus Symphony for Dummies*. Hoboken, NJ: Wiley Publishing, Inc., 2008.

University of Leeds Information Systems Services. "Spreadsheets." Retrieved August 2009 (http://iss.leeds.ac.uk/info/311/spreadsheets).

# INDEX

## A
automatic calculations, 11, 18
averages, determining, 11, 19–22

## B
Bricklin, Dan, 9

## C
cell reference, 18
cells, 18
    inserting/deleting, 27–28
charts/graphs, making in spreadsheets, 37
columns, 17–18
    inserting/deleting, 26–27
compatibility, and computer software, 13
constants, 25

## D
default formatting, changing, 29
digital librarian, questions to ask a, 30

## E
Excel, 11–12, 13, 15, 29, 37

## F
fonts, changing, 29
formula bar, 18
formulas, 18–22, 25
Frankston, Bob, 9
freeware, 15, 24

## G
geography, using spreadsheets for, 33–35
Google Docs, 15
grids, 17–18

## I
IBM, 11

## L
Landau, Remy, 8
LANPAR (Language for Programming Arrays at Random), 8–9
ledgers, 7
lists, using spreadsheets to make, 36–37
Lotus 1-2-3, 11, 13, 15

## M
Mattessich, Richard, 8
MAX/MIN functions, 22–23
menu bar, 16
Microsoft, 10, 11, 12, 13, 15

## P
paper worksheets, 7, 10–11
Pardo, Rene, 8

## Q
Quattro Pro, 13, 15, 37

# INDEX

## R
ranges, 20
rows, 17–18
    inserting/deleting, 26–27

## S
science, using spreadsheets for, 31–33
spreadsheets
    basics of, 16–23
    bundled with other software, 13, 24
    format and layout of, 28–29
    history of computerized, 8–12
    importance of knowing how to use, 13, 24, 38
    limits of, 23
    making changes to, 26–28
    myths and facts about, 24
    origin of name, 7
    questions to ask about, 30
    setting up, 25–29
    uses for, 31–38
    using for business, 6, 8–11, 12, 13, 23, 24, 37–38
    using for school, 4–6, 13, 23, 31–35, 37
    Web-based, 15, 24
suites, 13, 15, 24
SUM function, 22

## T
timetables, using spreadsheets to make, 36
toolbars, 16, 29

## V
values, 19–20, 22
VisiCalc, 9–10

## W
Web-based spreadsheets, 15, 24
what you see is what you get (WYSIWYG) interface, 10–11
width/height of cells, changing, 28–29
WordPerfect, 13, 15

## About the Author

Philip Wolny is a writer and editor from New York. Admittedly, Wolny was woefully under-schooled in spreadsheets upon finishing his undergraduate studies and had to scramble to catch up when he entered the job market. As a result, he feels especially grateful for the opportunity to help new learners enter the wide and wonderful world of spreadsheets.

## Photo Credits

Cover, p. 1 (left) © www.istockphoto.com/Nigel Carse; cover, p. 1 (second from left), p. 38 © www.istockphoto.com/Donald Gruener; cover, p. 1 (second from right) © www.istockphoto.com/Peter Zelei; cover, p. 1 (right) © www.istockphoto.com/Dimitrije Paunovic; pp. 5, 19, 27, 34 © Shutterstock; p. 8 Petrified Collection/Getty Images; p. 9 courtesy of Dan Bricklin, www.bricklin.com © www.jimraycroft.com 1982; p. 10 © courtesy of Dan Bricklin; p. 12 Richard Howard/Time-Life Pictures/Getty Images; p. 14 © AFP Photo/Gabriel Bouys/Newscom; p. 21 © David Young-Wolff/Photo Edit; p. 26 Yoshikazu Tsuno/AFP/Getty Images; p. 32 © Michael Newman/Photo Edit; p. 36 Ryan Anson/Getty Images.

Designer: Nicole Russo; Photo Researcher: Marty Levick